Coin Collecting

by MERVYN BENFORD

Ladybird Books Ltd   Loughborough   1976

Early money

An early form of buying and selling was *barter,* a system of exchanging goods. For example, a man might exchange food for something else he needed, perhaps a spear.

To Stone Age man, flint was a valuable rock found in chalk. Chalk is a rock found only in some areas. At Grimes Graves in Norfolk there was a Stone Age mine where men dug deep into the chalk to find the flint. They shaped it into useful tools and weapons which were taken all over the country to barter for other things they themselves needed.

In the Bronze and Iron Ages, people still bartered but had also discovered metals like copper, tin and iron. These metals were very useful. They could be melted down and made into many different useful and decorative articles. Because these metals were so valuable, people used them as money. Metal could be melted down and made into small bars. Bars were easier to store and keep safe. The safest place was often under the ground, and that is why old money is sometimes dug up by the machines of modern farmers and builders.

0 7214 0347 6

The first coins

When ·bartering, it was important to decide if one lot of goods was worth the others offered in exchange. The next idea was to agree to use objects like cattle as money, and in fact hundreds of things have been used in this way. Stone, salt, gunpowder and even slaves have served as money, but in time metal became more usual. Metal could be stamped to show its weight, which was its value. The King's head, or his name, could also be shown as proof of who had ordered the coins to be struck.

The Greeks were the first to strike coins as we would know them, around 800-600 BC. Early coins were not flat and round like ours, but more like lumps. In some countries, lumps of metal have been used until quite recent times. Bigger lumps or bigger coins (in the same metal) were more valuable because they weighed more. Names for coins sometimes came from the weights used, like the 'talents' and 'shekels' of the Bible. As time passed and skills improved, coins took on their more modern shapes.

The Frankish Emperor Charlemagne, in the 8th century AD, brought in a new currency in silver which became the pattern for many European countries. A pound weight of silver was divided into 240 smaller pieces and made into little coins which were called pennies. The old British £ s. d. system of counting money was based on 240 pennies making a pound, even when pennies could no longer be made in silver. We also had a weight called a pennyweight. Today coins of the same value all weigh the same and banks often count money by weighing it.

Half-tical

Above: Artist's impression of a Biblical scene showing money transactions in which talents and shekels would be used.

Inset above: Half-tical (Old Siamese unit of currency), a lump of silver weight/value stamped and used as money.

Below: Illustrating the relationship between weight and value in modern coins.

2 × 5p pieces = 1 × 10p piece

What coins can tell us

Usually the king or ruler ordered the issue of coins. Countries or cities which made coins were looked upon as important and kings became proud of their coins. Soon it became usual to put something on coins to show where they came from, usually the king's name and perhaps his head, or pictures of animals, birds, gods and goddesses. This side is called the *obverse,* while the 'tail' is known as the *reverse.* The value was usually on the reverse and the date might be on either. If there was room there might be other pictures of the country on the coin.

From coins we can learn of kings; of famous people, animals, birds and plants from many countries; of religions and of national symbols. British decimal coins have emblems of Scotland and of the Prince of Wales. St. George, killing the dragon, appears on British gold coins and silver crowns. Britannia first appeared on copper coins in King Charles II's reign, then on the silver fourpence of William IV and now on the 50p piece.

In 1965 Sir Winston Churchill, who died that year, became the first person other than the Sovereign to appear on British coins. Since then Prince Philip has been linked with the 1972 crown, or 25p coin, struck in silver and cupro-nickel in honour of the Queen's silver wedding. To celebrate Britain's entry into the Common Market there is now a special 50p piece.

Kossuth (Hungary)

Planck (West Germany)

Franco (Spain)

New Zealand Penny

West German Mark

Australian Penny

Irish Shilling

Irish 10p

United States 5 Cents

Great Britain Farthing

Canada 1 Cent

1972 Silver Wedding Crown

1965 Crown

More knowledge from coins

In 1937 Prince Albert became King George VI, and to honour his Scottish wife, Queen Elizabeth, it was decided to mint two kinds of shillings, one showing the English lion and the other the Scottish lion. The Scottish lion stands on its hind legs. These two separate shillings were still issued until the arrival of the new five-penny piece.

The words on a coin tell a story too. In 1947 full freedom was given to India, one of the colonies of the British Empire. The King could no longer call himself Emperor of India, and so, after 1948, British coins lost the letters IND. IMP. In 1521 Henry VIII was granted by the Pope the title 'Defender of the Faith'. Later, even though Henry broke away from the Roman Church, he kept the title and so have all British kings and queens since then. It is shown on our coins by the letters FID. DEF., an abbreviation from the Latin, or just F.D. The words on our coins, even the names, are usually in Latin form, but are not often written in full. 'BRITT. OMN.' was dropped in 1954 as more and more of our colonies became independent. Sometimes words appear on the edges of coins. This is an old idea which was at first an attempt to stop people clipping the edges of coins.

English Shillings

Scottish Shillings

1948 Penny
'Ind Imp' included

1949 Shilling 1949 Penny
'Ind Imp' omitted

1953 Halfpenny
'Britt Omn' included

1954 Halfpenny
'Britt Omn' omitted

Swedish 5 Crown piece
Specially minted for
500th Anniversary of
the Swedish Parliament

1 Franc: 1918

1 Franc: 1942

1 Franc: 1948

The making of coins—mints and mint marks

Coins are *struck* at a 'mint'. The Royal Mint was in the Tower of London until 1810, when a bigger mint was needed. It was built nearby.

In the days when travelling about was not always easy or safe, there were mints in several other parts of the country. Sample coins from these mints had to be sent to London for the weight and metal to be checked. Mints were owned by private firms who made large profits from their work. However, the King usually appointed men to watch over them. The Royal Mint also makes coins for many other countries. In 1968 a large new mint was built in South Wales.

In recent times the Royal Mint has minted almost all British coins. Several of the bronze coins in Victoria's reign, however, and some of the pennies in 1912, 1918 and 1919, were minted by Ralph Heaton and Sons of Birmingham. In 1918 and 1919, the Kings Norton Metal Company of Birmingham also helped with pennies. Heaton coins have a letter 'H' near the date and the others have 'KN'. The letters 'WW' and 'LCW' represent the Wyons, father and son, who were chief engravers at the Royal Mint in Victoria's reign. The initials of the designer have often appeared somewhere on our coins. There are still two private mints at Birmingham and they help the Royal Mint with overseas orders.

'Mint Marks'

William IV Farthing, 1831
The magnified view shows the
'WW' on the base of the neck

1874 'H' Farthing

1918 Penny

1918 'H' Penny

1918 'KN' Penny

Methods of making coins

Until the reign of Elizabeth I, British coins were always made by hand, hammered into shape and stamped while the metal was hot and soft. These coins were not always perfectly round and it was easy for people to cut or file the edges and make themselves rich with the shavings of silver and gold. Coin 'clippers' risked death or having their hands 'clipped', if they were caught! It is still against the law to damage, or deface, coins.

By 1662 more and more coins were being made on machines. Machines make coins to exact shapes, usually round, and can also put a 'milled' edge on the more valuable ones to stop their being clipped.

When coins are made today, the metal is first rolled into strips of the right thickness. Then the blank coins are cut out to the right shape and size. The edges are prepared and the designs are stamped on, using metal dies made from artists' drawings. Finally the coins are very carefully checked.

In 1937 the new 3d. piece was the first British coin not intended to be round. It had twelve sides. The British decimal 50-penny piece has seven slightly curved sides. It is an 'equilateral curve heptagon'. Unusual shapes help blind people, and people in the dark, to know what coin they have in their hand. All kinds of shapes have been tried by different countries. Some coins are made with a hole in the middle. This gives a bigger coin for less metal.

Milled and Plain edges

Two different shapes in British coins

1969 50p piece

1937 3d. piece

me coins that do not look quite round, but are !

Czechoslovakian korona coins

Some unusual shapes

Metals

Money has come in many forms but metal has been the more usual. The Greeks used gold and silver, metals which have been favoured ever since. These metals are scarce and this makes the coins valuable. Air, damp and dirt do not affect them. In time, less valuable coins were needed to help traders. Copper and bronze were used. Bronze is a mixture (alloy) of copper and tin. Lead, iron and nickel as well as many alloys have been used from earliest times. An alloy is not always an equal mixture.

The Romans added copper to gold to harden their coins and so make them last longer. Henry VIII added copper to silver, but only to save silver. Alloys have usually been used to help match the metal value with the face value of the coins. In recent years this has proved so difficult that it no longer matters; coins have become mere tokens. Choice of metal now has more to do with size, weight, colour and length of life.

A copper and zinc alloy gives a brass colour. Aluminium, aluminium-bronze or cupro-nickel are used to give a silver colour. Iron has been used in times of hardship but rusting was a problem. Coins of one metal may simply be coated with another, like a sandwich. Coins are now very much used in machines and the machines can only operate if a coin of the correct metal, weight and size has been used. Work continues on the use of new metals such as stainless iron and chrome iron.

erdigris a green impurity
copper, bronze and cupro-
kel

1891 Farthing
Staining on a new
bronze farthing

Gold

Half Sovereign

Copper

1839 Quarter Farthing

Silver

Bronze

upro-nickel
similar

uminium
similar

Coin collecting as a hobby

In the last few years many more people have begun to collect coins. Prices of good coins rose and are still quite high. More people looked at their change and found rare coins such as the 1933 penny and the Edward VIII threepence — even coins no one knew about, such as 1952 halfcrowns.

Nowadays we have paper money (banknotes) for large sums, instead of gold. At first these banknotes were promises to pay the actual value in coin if the owner wished. But this is no longer so. Coins are still used for amounts under a pound, but only for amounts that seem useful for buying and selling and giving change. We call these values *denominations*. We have had some very odd denominations but, like the farthing, and the halfpenny, they have been discontinued because their value became too small or too awkward to be useful, even after a change to cheaper metal. It is interesting to note that in the past pennies, halfpennies and farthings have all been struck in silver. The British halfcrown, three-penny piece and 'old' penny have gone because they did not fit the new decimal system.

1956 Farthing

1967 Halfcrown

1967 Halfpenny

Penny

Three-penny piece

Gold £5

Gold £1 Sovereign

Gold Half Sovereign

Collecting coins

A coin-collector is called a *numismatist.* His hobby is *numismatics.* The usual way to obtain coins for collection is by buying or exchanging. Some coins you need may appear in your change. Friends and relatives may give you some. There are clubs you may join where you can buy, sell and exchange. Some shops specialise in selling coins. It is a good idea to find one you like and get to know the dealer. He can help you very much. Take note of shops that pay more when buying. Such shops probably have higher selling prices. Coin fairs and auctions are other places worth visiting.

Good catalogues give details of small differences in design as well as dates when new designs appeared, or of mint marks and of numbers minted. A low mintage may mean rarity, but not always. Catalogues give an idea of the market value of coins.

A good dealer is your best friend when it comes to deciding the condition of a coin. This is a vital matter and something people easily disagree upon. The only sure way is to see a lot of coins, study them, talk to people and gradually learn what the different grades seem to be. Coin books and magazines, friends and club members may all be helpful but it is the dealer's opinion that matters most.

Special Proof Set, issued 1972 but dated 1970

Collecting coins:
Grades and conditions of coins

When a new design is decided upon, the Mint makes a special strike of *proof* coins. If a number of different coins have the new design, a *proof set* is produced. Proof coins are made from dies that are highly polished, with the design frosted to look dull. These coins are rare and minted in low numbers. From 1887 onwards they have been sold to collectors. Some or all of the new designs may appear the same year as ordinary coins and in normal numbers, but the 1951 Festival Crown was issued only in proof form. Proof coins are usually expensive, but a good investment. The special set on page 21 is a proof issue, a reminder of our old coins.

UNC. Uncirculated: Perfect coins showing no traces of wear, but with possibly a few slight marks made in minting. Coins made in millions on machines may suffer slight damage. Coins go to the banks in sealed Mint bags. A coin direct from such a bag is regarded as uncirculated.

B.U. Brilliant uncirculated: These are usually copper and bronze coins which still have their first brightness or *lustre.* This term may be used about silver coins, especially modern ones made of *cupro-nickel.*

F.D.C. Fleur-de-Coin: A perfect uncirculated coin with no marks.

In these grades the edge is as important as the head and tail.

1951 Crown (proof)

Note: The Maundy coins on p49 are also 'proof' condition. 1902 'proof' coins were made on metal blanks that were NOT highly polished — and are known as 'Matt Proof'.

Brilliant Uncirculated: (B.U.)

Uncirculated: (Unc.)
Not B.U.

Uncirculated, but made dark by the Mint:

1) to stop collectors hoarding the pennies because of their brightness;
2) to stop the farthings being passed as half-sovereigns.

More about grades and conditions

E.F. Extremely Fine: Such coins have been in circulation for only a short time. Slight traces of wear may show on the higher parts of the design, and B.U. coins may have lost some lustre, but otherwise these coins are close to new condition.

V.F. Very Fine: More coins are in this grade. They have been circulating longer and show wear on all the high parts. There may be slight cuts in the 'field' behind the design or tiny nicks in the edge. Under a magnifying glass they look less smooth. They are still good coins to collect and must be clean and very clear. No part of the main design should be lost and the hair in it should still show.

F. Fine: Even more wear, with some parts of the design lost. Nearly all the coins in your change will be in this grade or the next. Most of the coin will still be fairly clear, though not like V.F.

V.G. Very Good: Really rather poor, quite worn and with much of the design gone; the date and writing should still be clear. Perhaps half of all coins in circulation are F. or V.G. Extra letters in front of these grades help to split them up. 'A' means 'Almost', 'N' means 'Nearly' and 'G' means 'Good'. The two sides of a coin may not wear evenly and may be graded separately, e.g. E.F./V.F.

'E.F.'

'V.F.'

'F.'

'V.G.'

| Hair and wreath | Britannia's shoulder and knee | Hair and beard. Letters on neck | Flowers and rim. (These tails wear much better than the heads) |

A magnifying glass will help : Grading coins is very difficult,
there are many coins near these grades.
The high parts of the design wear first, usually before the words.

Care and storage of coins

Always take care of your coins. Keep them clean and dry. Hold them only by the edges. Silver coins in the best grades may be dipped in Silver Dip and/or washed in warm water with a *little* mild soap; in each case they need *well* rinsing and should be *lightly* dried (not rubbed) with a soft cloth. Brushing under water with an old, soft toothbrush may help with other coins but this is a risk with coins in the better grades. The golden rules are 'NEVER POLISH COINS' and 'CARE AND COMMON SENSE'. If you must try other methods, do not use your best coins. Think what you are doing and decide if it is worth the risk. A dealer may help you if a coin has a difficult stain, like green *verdigris* on copper and cupro-nickel.

To store coins, the following methods can be used: little plastic bags; small tubes to hold coins of the same kind; plastic pages with cards inside to hold a certain set of coins; plastic pages with pockets like the bags, but in different sizes and which fit into albums of different sizes; strong perspex cases, like trays, holding certain sets of coins; and finally cardboard albums with open pages, also like trays, to hold bigger sets. Buy what suits you.

Sets

It is difficult to cover a very wide range of coins in a collection. Most collectors decide to collect in sets. A set may be made up in a number of ways according to the choice of the collector.

The following are two kinds of sets which do not need coins from every year.

TYPE SETS: A Type Set shows one of each different type of whatever coins you are collecting. It may be just one kind of coin, such as a shilling, or coins of just one reign, such as Queen Victoria's. Instead of having one from each year you need only one of each sort. A Type Set must show any change of design, or of head, or words, or perhaps of metal, and such changes may be shown on just one coin or a whole set, like the IND. IMP. change on British coins in 1947.

YEAR SETS: For these sets, specimens of all the coins of one year are collected. Then another year is chosen and so on. Modern coins are good for this purpose. Collecting years where there have been new coins, or changes of coin, is a way to mix type-collecting with year-collecting. The coins in sets should be of the same grade if possible.

Elizabeth II Year Set 1953

(A 1902 Year Set is also the full Edward VII Type Set)

Type Set
of Bronze Farthings
These 11 coins cover all
the types. Some
collectors use extra coins
to show Heads
and Tails together.

British coins before Queen Victoria

Iron Age British tribes used some Greek and Roman coins but soon began to make their own. More Roman coins came during the Roman occupation. Spanish coins found at Hadrian's Wall show that at the date on the coins troops from Rome's Spanish colonies manned the wall.

The Roman words 'libra', 'solidus' and 'denarius', gave us the '£ s. d.' for our own pounds, shillings and pence. Pounds and shillings were not at first actual coins, being used only for counting, but we have had pennies since Saxon times, first in silver, then copper and now bronze.

Tudor Kings were the first to strike shillings. The gold sovereign and guinea changed value often but later settled at a pound and twenty-one shillings. Gold coins have not been used as money since George V's reign, though some have been minted for collectors and museums. Coins were not issued every year. The George III 'cartwheel' 1d. and 2d. were made only in 1797. If real coins ran short, towns, and even traders, made their own, called tokens. Coins have been made which were worth (old money) 1½d., 1/8, 3/4, 6/8, 7/-, 15/- and some worth only a quarter, third or half of a farthing.

Roman coins are fairly easy to come by but otherwise, up to about 1700, a collector may find most British coins rare and expensive. From William III onwards it may be possible to find enough coins to make up Type Sets.

1797
Cartwheel 2d.
George III

Some older
British coins

'Penny Token'

½ Farthing 1844   ⅓ Farthing 1902   ¼ Farthing 1839

George II Shilling and Sixpence

George III   George IV   William IV
                    Copper Farthings

Coins of Queen Victoria's reign: 1837-1901
Copper and Bronze

Queen Victoria's reign gave us many coins and is a good reign for the collector. There were enough changes to make even a Type Set a problem. Hers is the first reign from which coins are still fairly plentiful, though some are now expensive even when in poor condition. The coins date from 1838. Some dates were over-stamped by the Mint with a later one (such as 1862 changed to 1865) and to spot these, like the Mint letters on some coins, you may need a magnifying glass.

After 1860, copper became too valuable to use and smaller coins made of bronze were minted instead, though copper coins and bronze coins were both minted in 1860. The 'Young' or 'Bun' head lasted till 1895, when the 'Old' or 'Veiled' head replaced it, though in that year 'Young' and 'Old' farthings appeared. The 'Bun' head was, at times, changed in detail very slightly during its long life. In 1860 the new bronze coins came with a beaded edge as well as the more usual toothed edge.

Queen Victoria

Victoria

1860 Bronze

Round beads
at edge

Toothed beads
at edge

Bronze Types

Young Head

Farthing

Halfpenny

Penny

Old Head

Farthing

Halfpenny

Penny

Silver coins of Queen Victoria's reign: 1837-1901

Victorian silver coins are interesting. The first florin in 1849 (see page 46) had the letters 'D.G.' omitted from the Queen's titles. The Gothic florin came in 1851 but only 1,540 were minted that year so they are very rare. All 'Young Head' halfcrowns are expensive, as there are not very many to collect. For Jubilee Year a special double-florin was struck but it was not liked and lasted only four years. The silver groat, or fourpence, with Britannia on the reverse, had re-appeared in 1836 and continued to be minted for a while.

By 1887 the Queen had reigned for fifty years. On all silver and gold coins a new head, the *'Jubilee Head'*, appeared. It lasted till 1893 when the 'Old Head' took over. In 1887 both heads were used and in 1893 the threepence, sixpence and shilling came in each Type. In 1889 the shilling's Jubilee head was made larger. Jubilee coins make good Type and Year Sets. Like the 1895 farthings, where two heads come in the same year, the earlier one is more valuable. The 'Young Head' on the sixpence was slightly changed in 1867 and 1880. The reverse of the 1887 Jubilee sixpence was changed the same year, since if gilded, it could be made to look very like the half-sovereign.

Queen Victoria

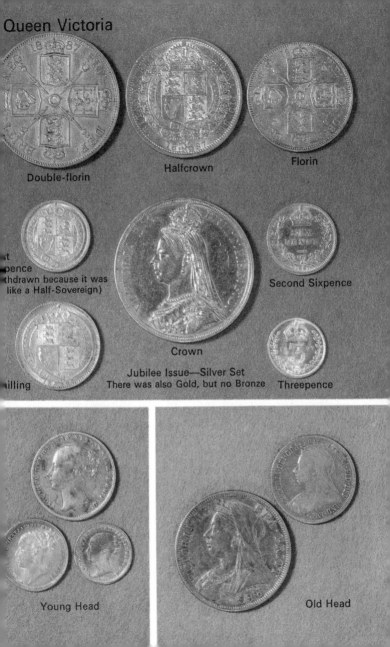

Double-florin

Halfcrown

Florin

...t
...pence
...thdrawn because it was
like a Half-Sovereign)

Second Sixpence

...illing

Crown

Jubilee Issue—Silver Set
There was also Gold, but no Bronze

Threepence

Young Head

Old Head

Coins of King Edward VII's reign: 1902-1910

King Edward's reign was short, but the nine different coins needed to make a full set are each quite valuable. Even a Type Set in good condition will prove expensive. Most coins come in only one Type. Gold coins, crowns and the third-farthing came only in 1902. Also in 1902 there were two Types of pennies and halfpennies, known as *High* and *Low Tide* because of the level of the sea on the reverse. 1910 may be the best chance of a Year Set because of the number of coins minted. 1902 makes an interesting Year Set because it is also a full Type Set.

The third-farthing was minted for use in Malta. Most coins worth less than a farthing had for some years been minted only for use in the Colonies. Other British coins were of course used there and the sixpences of 1952 were all sent to the West Indies. From 1897 to 1917 all farthings had been blackened by the Mint to stop people passing these bright little coins as half-sovereigns. Half-sovereigns were not coined after 1917. Crowns were no longer used much as money. 1903-05 are difficult years for silver, especially halfcrowns. Only 166,008 were minted in 1905.

Coins of George V's reign: 1911-1936

A Type Set of this reign will be a fairly full one. The 'H' and 'KN' pennies have been mentioned but the main change concerned the 'heads' used. The first 'head' was slightly changed on the halfpenny in 1925. This 'modified effigy' ('M.E.') was used on the other coins in 1926. In 1928 a third, smaller, 'head' was used on the pennies and halfpennies, while the silver coins were given a new 'tail' in 1927. The 'tail' design of the bronze coins remained as Britannia, but slight differences came at about the time of the 'modified head'. In certain cases, the two earlier heads both appeared in the year of the change (that is, 1925 and 1926). There are therefore coins which bear the same date but on which the head is different.

In 1920 an alloy containing only half silver was used for the first time, and by 1925 'silver' coins were no longer made of pure silver. There were no special coins for King George V's coronation, except the Proof Sets. Crowns were not minted until the new coinage of 1928, when a few were made each year for collectors until 1934 and then again in 1936. In 1935 a special crown honoured the twenty-fifth year of the King's reign. The reign saw the very rare 1933 penny, of which only a dozen were minted. At least three have never been found.

1925: Modified

1926: Modified
B.M. on neck moved and no dots

Blackened

Coins of Edward VIII's reign: 1936-1937 and George VI's reign: 1937-1952

Despite the use of George V's head, coins of 1936 are really within Edward's reign. He gave up the throne before coins bearing his own head could be issued, but work had begun on the new twelve-sided 'brass' threepences. Twelve were sent to a slot-machine firm for testing and five of these have still to be found. These coins have Edward's head facing left, breaking the custom of changing the direction with each new king. The head of George VI, his brother, also faces left.

All coins except the penny and shilling received new tails. The extra Scottish shilling was minted and also the new 'brass' threepence. The silver threepence was issued as well until 1945. In 1947 'silver' coins lost even their half silver and were made in cupro-nickel. 1949 saw the loss of 'IND. IMP.' from all coins, and the introduction of a second new tail for the sixpence. There was a crown in 1937 and the special Proof one in 1951 for the Festival of Britain. There were enough pennies in circulation in 1949 and so very few were minted in 1950 and 1951. The King died in 1952 and only farthings, halfpennies, threepences and sixpences were thought to have been minted and issued. The two halfcrowns found in change in recent years were a real surprise to collectors.

Change of metal
after 1946

No 'Ind Imp
from 1949

Coins of Elizabeth II's reign: 1953-

Our present Queen's reign promises to be a long one and decimal currency will be the biggest change her coins will show. A new head has been drawn for them and completely new reverse designs. Britannia moved to the 50p. To stop people hoarding the 'last' of the old coins, the Mint decided to give the one date, 1967, to all coins struck during the three years from 1967-70. The last shillings were struck in 1966. The special Proof set of old coins shown on page 21 was dated 1970 but not issued until after the change to decimal currency. So only the 6d., 1/- and 2/- could ever legally have been spent.

Pennies were still plentiful in 1953 and none were issued before 1961, except for those in Coronation sets. One test penny dated 1954 somehow escaped from the Mint and has been found. Coronation coins came as usual in Proof and Cased sets, but there was also a special set, without the crown, in a plastic holder. All Coronation Year coins still had 'BRITT. OMN.' but this was dropped in 1954.

Farthings were not made after 1956. In 1960 a crown was struck, though for no special reason. 1965 saw the Churchill crown, and in 1972 came the Silver Wedding crown, our first 25p coin. Some of the 1972 crowns were struck in silver and they are already very valuable. In 1973 came the special 50p coin in honour of Britain's entry into the Common Market. No ordinary coins were struck in 1972.

lizabeth II

cial 50p commemorating
ish entry to the
mon Market.

1953 Plastic Souvenir Set (no Crown).
Full set, with Crown, shown on P29.

GREAT BRITAIN
1960
EIIR   EIIR

HALF CROWN

THREEPENCE

CROWN

FLORIN

ENGLISH
SHILLING

SIXPENCE

SCOTTISH
SHILLING

HALF PENNY

960 Set in perspex box.
ote: No pennies 1954–1960.
965 and 1972 are other Elizabeth Year Sets with Crowns.

Decimal currency

For hundreds of years Britain counted money using a system called Pounds, Shillings and Pence. Twelve pence made a shilling and twenty shillings a pound, though there have not always been coins worth these amounts.

On February 15th, 1971, a change was made to *decimal currency.* A decimal system uses ten or a hundred of the smaller units to make the larger one. There are only Pounds and Pence in the new system and 100 Pence equal one Pound. Most countries of the world, and especially those in Europe, use a decimal system.

There are now six coins: halfpenny, penny and twopence in bronze (brown); fivepence, tenpence and fiftypence in cupro-nickel (silvery). After a few years the halfpenny will become too low in value to be useful and will disappear. Full sets were issued, for collectors, before February 1971 but could not be used for spending until later. The 5p and 10p coins were put into circulation as early as 1968, as they exactly matched the old shilling and florin. The 50p coin was introduced in 1969 to replace the ten shilling note.

Special sets of the new coins (except the 50p) were issued in 1968. Bronze coins were dated 1971, the year of the change.

The last old coins (normal issue) 1967 and the first new ones 1968, 1969, 1971.
Note: No shillings in 1967.
1972 special set was not a normal issue.

The need for new coins

Decimal coinage is not a new idea. In 1849 a new coin worth two shillings was minted. It was called 'One Tenth of a Pound', to show it was a decimal coin, and it replaced the halfcrown. Later it took the name of 'Florin'. From 1851 it had the date in Roman numerals and the words in Gothic script, a kind of writing long in use, especially in Germany. The country did not change to decimal currency, and the halfcrown returned in 1874. However, people liked the florin and it was not withdrawn. It still remains as the new ten-penny piece, and is still worth one tenth of a pound.

Often, after a war, changes in the value of money and the cost of metal may make it necessary to introduce new coins. France and Russia altered their money in recent years, and Hungary has had three different currencies this century. During the last war Sweden ran short of copper but had plenty of iron, so 'copper' coins were made of iron, despite the problem of rust. The Americans tried steel coins coated with zinc for the same reason. Such changes tell part of a country's history.

Gothic Florin
Note: Date in Roman numerals

Gothic Florin
One Florin = $\frac{1}{10}$ of a pound

Finland 1 Markka 10 Markkaa
Before 1963

1 Penni   10 Pennia
After 1963

...ia 1 Kopeck 1897   1 Kopeck 1961

France 100 Franc 1955
100 Francs became 1 New Franc in 1959

...pper

Sweden 5 Ore   2 Ore   1 Ore

Iron

Change to Iron during war years, notice rusting.

Maundy money

Maundy Thursday, the day before Good Friday, is the day when we remember the last supper Jesus gave to his disciples, and when he washed their feet to show he did not think himself more important than they. From early times kings and popes and bishops have washed the feet of the poor on this day each year. In England the king washed the feet of as many poor men as he was years old and gave them money, food and clothing.

In time this custom grew less popular. Elizabeth I had the people's feet washed and spiced first by her servants. James II was the last to do the job himself. William III had nothing to do with the washing at all and from 1754 the Maundy Service became only a gift of money. Special silver pennies, twopences, threepences and fourpences, first used by Charles II, are still minted and are the only part of the old custom now left. The rest of the gift is made up with ordinary money, and comes in rather attractive little leather bags. Maundy money is still minted according to the age of the king or queen. The sets of Maundy coins are quite rare. The values are now new pence.

Proof set of Maundy
coins (above)

Maundy coins totalling 37 pence, (right)
part of the Maundy money
given to a recipient in 1963.
The rest of the money was given in cash.

Leather bags contained the Maundy coins,
the ordinary money and a 1953 Crown.

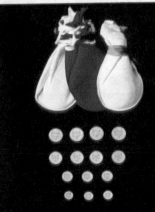

Treasure

Anyone who finds a buried hoard of gold or silver, or of coins, must by law report it as 'Treasure Trove'. A special Court decides if the finder may keep it, but if it must go to the Crown the finder is usually given its value in money. 'Treasure Trove' is usually old. Here is a list of the scarcer 'treasure', or better years, to look for in modern coins. Not all of these coins are as rare as each other and some are rare only in top grades. The list shows some of the better dates of each reign. Most Victorian silver is rare: Elizabeth issues should be 'UNC'.

The 1860 *copper* issues are very valuable.

Farthings: 1863, 1875, 1876H, 1892, 1895YH, 1904, 1910-15, 1935, 1938, 1956.

Halfpennies: 1864, 1869, 1871, 1902LT, 1904, 1913, 1925-27, 1946, 1954-56.

Pennies: 1864, 1867-71, 1875H, 1902LT, 1904, All H and KN, 1926, 1926ME, 1932-34, 1940-46, 1950-51, 1953.

Threepences: 1849, 1855, 1887YH, 1893JH, 1904-06, 1926-30, 1942-44 (Brass: 1946, 1949-51).

Sixpences: 1848, 1854, 1862-63, 1867, 1882, 1893JH, 1904-05, 1917, 1923, 1938, 1952, 1954-56.

Shillings: 1848, 1850-51, 1854, 1862-63, 1867, 1882, 1889SH, 1903-05, 1913, 1925, 1930, 1934, 1938, 1958E, 1959S, 1961S.

Florins: 1851, 1854, 1862-63, 1867, 1891-92, 1903-05, 1909, 1924-25, 1932, 1954.

Halfcrowns: 1839-50, 1879, 1887YH, 1903-10, 1924-25, 1926ME, 1930, 1932, 1934, 1938, 1958-59.

Rare or Difficult Coins

1950

1882

1904

1910

1930

1946

1946

1949

Remember: Some common dates are rare in Uncirculated, or even E.F. condition, and some rare coins are hard to find in these grades.

THE REIGNS OF SOME EUROPEAN MONARCHS

AUSTRIA (incl. Hungary)

Francis I 1804-35
Ferdinand I .. 1835-48
Franz Joseph 1848-1916
Carl I 1916-18

BELGIUM

Leopold I 1831-65
Leopold II .. 1865-1909
Albert I.. 1909-34
Leopold III
.. .. .. 1934-45, 1950-51
Baudouin 1951-

BULGARIA

Alexander II .. 1879-86
Ferdinand I 1887-1918
Boris III 1918-43
Simeon II 1943-46

DENMARK

Frederick VI .. 1808-39
Christian VIII .. 1839-48
Frederick VII .. 1848-63
Christian IX 1863-1906
Frederick VIII .. 1906-12
Christian X.. .. 1912-47
Frederick IX .. 1947-72
Margrethe II .. 1972-

FRANCE

Louis XVIII.. .. 1814-24
Charles X 1824-30
Louis Philippe .. 1830-48
Napoleon III .. 1852-70

GERMANY

Friedrich Wilhelm III
.. .. 1797-1840
Friedrich Wilhelm IV
.. .. 1840-61
Wilhelm I 1861-88
Friedrich III .. 1888
Wilhelm II .. 1888-1918

GREECE

Otto 1831-63
George I .. 1863-1913
Constantine I
.. .. .. 1913-17, 1920-22
Alexander 1917-20
George II 1922-24, 1935-47
Paul I 1947-64
Constantine II .. 1964-71

ITALY

Vittorio Emanuele II
.. .. 1861-78
Umberto I .. 1878-1900
Vittorio Emanuele III
.. .. 1900-46
Umberto II.. .. 1946